Unforgettable Hollywood

UNFORGETTABLE

HOLLYWOOD

Nat Dallinger

William Morrow and Company, Inc.
New York   1982

Library of Congress Cataloging in Publication Data

Dallinger, Nat.
   Unforgettable Hollywood.

   1. Moving-picture actors and actresses—United
States—Portraits.   I. Title.
PN1998.A2D35   791.43′028′0922   82-3479
ISBN: 0-688-01323-6   AACR2

Printed in the United States of America

 2 3 4 5 6 7 8 9 10

Book Design by Leslie Achitoff

To my wife, Harriet, for her loving persuasion and assistance. Also, for our daughter, Toni, and her husband, Gerry, for their confidence and welcome encouragement.

Publisher's Note

Nat Dallinger was born in Baltimore in 1911. Following the death of his mother in 1922, he and his father moved to Southern California, where he has lived ever since.

In 1932, while accompanying his photographer-brother on an assignment to cover a rodeo at the Los Angeles Coliseum, he grew fascinated with the work. Borrowing a camera, he ventured into Hollywood, where he began to take candid pictures of screen stars at such traditional hangouts as the Brown Derby and the Cocoanut Grove.

Soon he was selling his photographs to the leading news-picture syndicates. He became a staff photographer with *The New York Times* photo syndicate, Wide World Photos, and then headed its Hollywood bureau.

Five years later he joined the publicity staff at Metro-Goldwyn-Mayer studios and for a short time helped publicize the stars under contract there, among them Clark Gable, Robert Taylor, Spencer Tracy, Joan Crawford, Norma Shearer, Elizabeth Taylor, Judy Garland, and Mickey Rooney.

But when he became unhappy with studio restrictions, he left MGM and spent the next several years taking photographs for national magazines and news-picture syndicates.

In 1941, he created the first by-line photo feature service from Hollywood when he contracted with the *Daily News* in Chicago to supply a weekly feature that was given two pages in rotogravure each Saturday.

Finally, two years later, Nat Dallinger joined King Features Syndicate, which allowed worldwide distribution of his photographs. These were taken not only at the major studios but also at parties, nightclubs, and, in particular, in the homes of their screen-star subjects, which may account for their unique candidness, informality, and warmth.

Mr. Dallinger has been retired for several years. *Unforgettable Hollywood*, the first collection of his work, has been arranged and captioned by himself.

The Rare Ones

(1960)   JUDY GARLAND and PRESIDENT JOHN F. KENNEDY, pictured
in a happy mood during dinner at a Democratic National Con-
vention fund-raising event at the Hilton Hotel in Beverly Hills. A
frequent visitor to Southern California, the late President was fond
of many screen personalities and often met them at the home of his
sister Pat (Mrs. Peter Lawford) in Santa Monica, on the Pacific
Ocean.

(1964) GEORGE MURPHY (*left*) was an interested bystander as PRESIDENT DWIGHT D. EISENHOWER was interviewed by reporters. Occasion was a testimonial dinner for United States Senator-elect Murphy, veteran star of motion pictures, at the Hollywood Palladium. Ike was always welcome in Hollywood and a favorite golfing partner at Palm Springs, nearby desert playspot and home of many movie stars.

(1960)   MILTON BERLE (*left*) and then-Senator LYNDON B. JOHNSON. Never at a loss for words as a general rule, Berle appears to be groping for an appropriate remark in this photo at a Democratic fund-raising event in Hollywood. Despite his witty barbs at the expense of high government dignitaries, Berle has often been invited to entertain them.

(1959) THE DUKE AND DUCHESS OF WINDSOR being feted in Hollywood. On their initial visit to the film capital—as they toured California—the former King of England and his Maryland-born wife had a ball at a star-studded dinner party hosted by Cobina Wright, late newspaper society columnist. Edward, Duke of Windsor, was highly amused by the dancing antics of the Duchess, the lady for whom he abdicated the throne of England—in 1937. A rare photograph.

(1961) FORMER PRESIDENT RICHARD M. NIXON (*right*) shown with JACK BENNY at an American-Israel Foundation dinner in Beverly Hills, honoring the comedy star for his activities in behalf of the Foundation's cultural exchange program—and for his contributions toward the building of the Tel Aviv Cultural Center, home of the Israel Philharmonic Orchestra. Nixon presented Benny with an award for his fine work.

(1935) SHIRLEY TEMPLE displays one of her proudest possessions, an autographed photo from Franklin Delano Roosevelt, President of the United States. One of FDR's favorite entertainers, the former child star later gained additional fame serving in high government positions here and abroad. All-time worldwide favorite child screen star, the California-born actress was among the top box-office grossers during most of her film career.

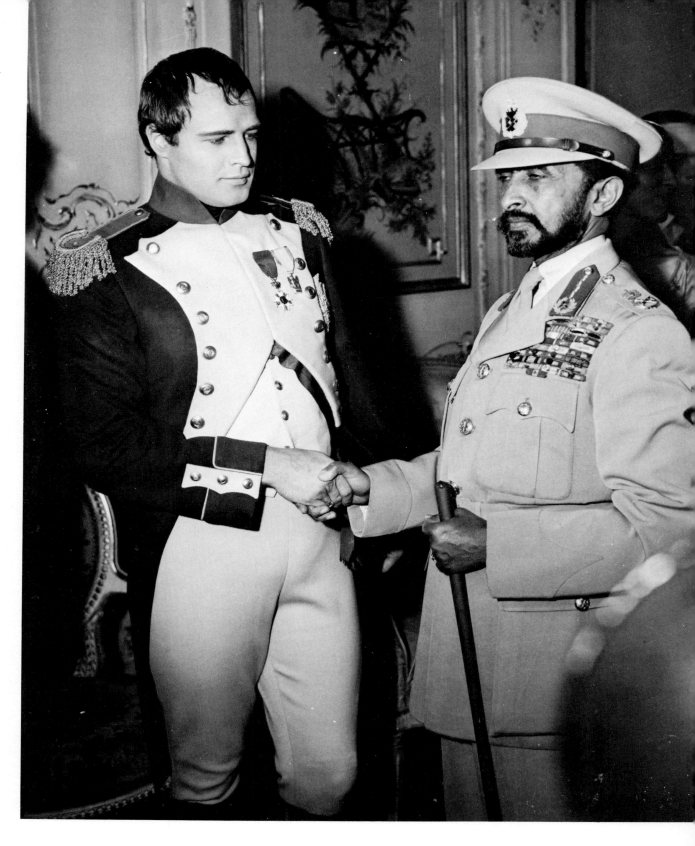

(1954) HAILE SELASSIE (*right*), late Emperor of Ethiopia, and MARLON BRANDO, dressed for his role of Napoleon, on the sound-stage set of *Desirée*. The two met during the former's visit to the movie capital. A motion-picture fan, the Emperor viewed films regularly at his palace in Addis Ababa. Brando appears to be admiring the many decorations worn by Emperor Selassie.

(1958) YUL BRYNNER, LORD LOUIS MOUNTBATTEN and MARGARET LEIGHTON (*from left to right*) during a brief visit to Hollywood by Britain's top naval officer and uncle of Prince Philip Mountbatten, Queen Elizabeth's husband. Production on the pictures being filmed ceased when the stars left their sets to meet the heroic visitor, lovingly referred to by members of his family as "Dickie." Obviously admiring Miss Leighton (a native of Worcestershire, England), Lord Louis may not have been aware that Yul Brynner—with hair—was a rare sight.

(1952) ETHEL BARRYMORE and her brother, LIONEL BARRYMORE, members of one of the most illustrious theatrical families (their father was the renowned actor, Maurice Barrymore), attend a Hollywood social function. Both were born in Philadelphia, where Ethel attended a convent before making her stage debut at the age of fifteen. She was awarded an Oscar for her performance in *None but the Lonely Heart*. Multi-talented Lionel, too, was an Oscar winner, for his performance in *A Free Soul*, and he composed music and was a fine etcher.

(1936)   JOHN BARRYMORE wears a stern expression during a court appearance in Los Angeles. John was one of the most popular stars of stage and screen, often referred to as "The Profile," but his marital record was less successful. Along with his excellent screen portrayals, the Philadelphia-born star's stage performances of *Hamlet* served as a course in acting for other aspiring actors. John was a few years younger than his equally renowned brother and sister, Lionel and Ethel. The three Barrymores appeared together only once, in the movie *Rasputin and the Empress*. Before turning to the stage, John had sought a career as a cartoonist.

(1936) CLARK GABLE and wife CAROLE LOMBARD attend a sports
event. She was at the height of her motion-picture career when she
met a tragic death in an airplane crash. The Indiana-born actress
started acting at age twelve, later attracting considerable attention as
a Mack Sennett bathing beauty. It was soon after her death that
Gable forsook Hollywood to serve with the armed forces. It helped
alleviate his suffering.

(1948) BING CROSBY and wife DIXIE, dining out in Hollywood. Dixie was mother of Bing's four oldest sons; her death in 1952 was a great shock to all. She, too, was a vocalist, known as Dixie Lee. Several years elapsed before Bing wed again, becoming the husband of actress Kathryn Grant, mother of his three younger children.

(1949)   ROBERTO ROSSELLINI, INGRID BERGMAN and her husband,
DR. PETER LINDSTROM (*from left to right*), became central figures in
newspaper headlines shortly after this photo was snapped at a
Hollywood theater. Rossellini, one of Italy's best-known film direc-
tors, was fortunate to have Ingrid appear as the leading lady of a
projected new motion picture. What the doctor—and all of Hollywood—did not anticipate was that she would also fall in love with
the director, divorce her husband and seek new happiness as Mrs.
Rossellini. This marriage also failed, and the Swedish-born actress
sought wedded bliss elsewhere.

(1943) ROBERT WALKER, his wife, JENNIFER JONES, and DAVID O. SELZNICK, film producer (*from left to right*). Happily wed at the time of this photo and the parents of two sons, Bob and Jennifer divorced in 1945, a few years before his untimely death. The Oklahoma-born actress was awarded an Oscar for her title role in *The Song of Bernadette*, and starred in numerous other important films.

(1957) ELIZABETH TAYLOR and her husband, MIKE TODD, were joined by their very dear friend, singer EDDIE FISHER, at a Hollywood restaurant. Widowed by the death of Todd as a result of an airplane crash in 1958, the glamorous actress became Fisher's bride the following year. He became her ex-husband when Richard Burton won her love.

(1953) JOE DIMAGGIO (*left*) and WALTER WINCHELL, a pair of headliners. Joe's name is indelibly inscribed in baseball records as one of the greatest players ever to swing a bat. Winchell, shown with Joe at a benefit baseball game in Los Angeles, made history as a newspaper, radio and television columnist. His broadcasts kept followers glued to their radios and TVs throughout the many years he dispensed the very latest news to "Mr. and Mrs. America—and all the ships at sea"—his customary opening words.

(1945) CARY GRANT and wife BARBARA HUTTON in one of the few photos ever snapped of them. Reputed to be "the world's richest woman," Barbara was camera-shy, preferring to remain in the background, and leave the limelight to her equally famous actor husband.

(1954) JAMES DEAN and actress PIER ANGELI at a Hollywood party. A remarkable, now legendary young actor, Dean was just twenty-four years old when an automobile crash ended his life. Pier, born in Sardinia, Italy, won a Hollywood screen contract after appearing in films in her native country.

(1945) CHARLES CHAPLIN and wife OONA in front-row seats at a
tennis tournament—their favorite sport. The famous comedian was
a top tennis player and often hosted matches at his Beverly Hills
home. Aside from his unforgettable comedy performances, the
London-born actor also excelled as a director, producer, writer and
composer.

(1936) JEAN HARLOW, one of the first of the screen's "blond bombshells," lived for just one more year following this photo showing her vacationing at a coastal resort a short distance from Hollywood. Only twenty-six at the time of her death, the Missouri-born actress was particularly entertaining in those pictures in which she costarred with Clark Gable.

(1957) LANA TURNER and her boyfriend, JOHNNY STOMPANATO, garnered reams of space in gossip columns during their brief period of steady dating. Unfortunately, his somewhat mysterious death in the home of the actress ended that romantic association for the blond screen star. As ruggedly handsome as many screen Romeos, Johnny, a World War II veteran, was the owner of a gift shop.

(1943) MADAME CHIANG KAI-SHEK, seated beside film producer DAVID O. SELZNICK, was the honored guest at a fund-raising dinner at Hollywood's Ambassador Hotel. Widow of the general who played a major role in the modern history of China, Madame Chiang is reported to be a resident of Long Island, New York.

(1950) VIVIEN LEIGH and CLARK GABLE, *Gone With the Wind*'s famous costars, were table companions at an after-theater party in Beverly Hills. Teaming this pair in the romantic, excitement-filled motion picture was possibly the most brilliant casting ever done in Hollywood. The smash box-office grosser set new records for both attendance and financial returns, exceeded only by a few films in recent years. Both are gone, but never forgotten: SCARLETT O'HARA and RHETT BUTLER.

(1934) GRETA GARBO did her utmost to avoid being photographed in a solo appearance at Shrine Auditorium in Los Angeles, but to no avail. The best the actress could do was supply the photographer with a near-perfect candid shot.

The War Years-
World War II

(1943) GEORGE RAFT is best remembered as a tough guy, having enacted many such roles in motion pictures. However, the multitalented New Yorker was a fancy-dancing vaudevillian before donning greasepaint for his screen appearances. Shown displaying his terpsichorean expertise, Raft delighted in entertaining members of the armed forces at every opportunity.

(1943)   JUDY GARLAND sang her heart out for GIs at the Hollywood Canteen, devoting much of her free time to entertaining the servicemen, who were either in transit or on brief liberty from active duty. Beloved by admirers throughout the world, the petite song star began life as Frances Gumm, in Grand Rapids, Minnesota.

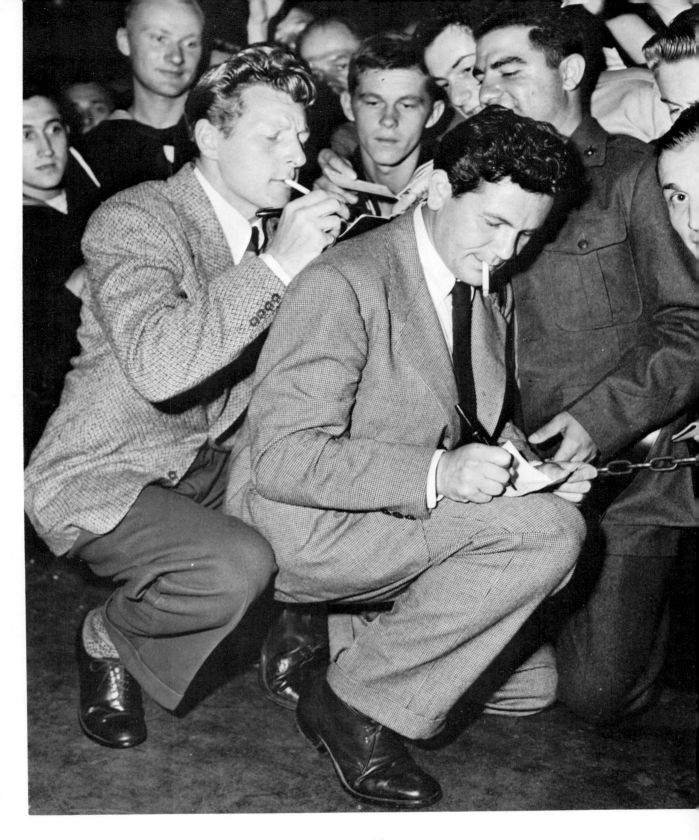

(1944) DANNY KAYE uses JOHN GARFIELD's back in this double-decker autographing session at the Hollywood Canteen. Demand for signatures of the stars at the recreational center was so great, celebrities often developed writer's cramp. With Bette Davis, Garfield helped create the Canteen. Together they recruited a host of other notables to share the endless chores at the servicemen's haven.

(1945) NORMA SHEARER and her husband, NAVAL LIEUTENANT MARTI ARROUGE, dance away an evening during a brief liberty period for the test pilot. The interesting hairdo worn by the actress is one of many created just for her but soon copied by admiring fans everywhere. Heart-shaped rings worn by this couple were inscribed with "Everything leads me to thee," a line from *Romeo and Juliet.*

(1944) BURGESS MEREDITH, an air force captain in World War II, checks ticket stubs with his actress wife, PAULETTE GODDARD. The well-liked actor and his beautiful wife were married a short time before this photograph was taken. Paulette was a model before becoming an actress, and her outstanding beauty attracted the attention of Florenz Ziegfeld, which resulted in her stage debut in one of his fabulous reviews.

(1945) DANE CLARK (*left*) and RODDY MCDOWALL were among the
many prominent screen personalities to help out nightly at the
Hollywood Canteen. Believe it or not, milk was the number one
drink requested by the servicemen.

(1944) VICTOR MATURE is the attentive coastguardsman shown
lighting a cigarette for his glamorous companion, actress CAROLE
LANDIS, during a short leave between stops of a bond-selling tour.
Born in Louisville, Kentucky, Mature was one of many film leading
men to graduate to motion pictures from the Pasadena Playhouse, a
few miles from Hollywood.

Party Time

(1958) JOANNE WOODWARD and husband PAUL NEWMAN dressed as British "Westerners" for the Share Inc. ball at the Cocoanut Grove. Thomasville, Georgia, was the birthplace of this fine actress, winner of an Oscar for her brilliant performance in *The Three Faces of Eve*. During World War II, Newman spent three years in the Pacific as a radio operator on naval torpedo planes.

(1950)   SHELLEY WINTERS (*left*) and ANN BLYTH are the costumed actresses at this Hollywood party. Shelley attended as a harp-playing angel, Ann as Sadie Thompson, a well-known character of stage and screen stories. A talented stage as well as screen actress, Shelley has won two Oscars. Ann made her acting debut on radio at the age of five—in her native New York.

(1948)   DOROTHY MALONE is the actress with DR. PHILIP MONTGOM-
ERY in (believe it or not) this shower outfit at the Hollywood Press
Photographers' Costume Ball. The shower, attached to the doctor's
back, in no way impeded the couple's dancing at the party. Academy
Award winner Dorothy's participation in high school acting compe-
titions started her career in Chicago, her hometown.

(1946) JACKIE COOPER and his actress wife, JUNE HORNE. A former child screen star, Jackie here is shown as Skippy, a role he made famous in films. Born in Los Angeles, he served with the United States Navy in World War II. His acting credits include numerous stage and television appearances. One of his finest screen portrayals was opposite Wallace Beery in *The Champ*.

(1949) ROCK HUDSON and VERA-ELLEN startled everyone at the Hollywood Press Photographers' Costume Ball when they appeared as Mr. and Mrs. Academy Award Oscar, totally covered with gilt paint. Their makeup, which took three hours to remove after the party, brought the greatest applause from the gathering. The actress danced her way to screen popularity. Along with his successful career in motion pictures, Rock also enjoyed high rating as the star of TV's *McMillan and Wife*.

(1948)   ROSALIND RUSSELL (*left*) and LORETTA YOUNG wore identical outfits to the Photographers' Costume Ball, an annual event which was unquestionably "the top party of the year." Although these glamorous stars vied for top acting honors in the same year, the award going to Loretta for her title role in *The Farmer's Daughter*, in real life they were the best of friends.

(1947) EDGAR BERGEN and his wife, FRANCES, dressed as two of the famed ventriloquist's brainchildren, Charlie McCarthy and Mortimer Snerd, for their appearance at the Photographers' Costume Ball. Frances (Westerman) forsook her own acting career when she became Mrs. Bergen, assisting Edgar in his act and at the same time bringing up their talented daughter, Candice.

(1948) JANE RUSSELL was an eye-pleasing treat for patrons at a benefit show in Hollywood, appearing in this abbreviated costume. After she was discovered by Howard Hughes, famed flyer and aircraft builder, Jane's pinup photos skyrocketed her to fame with her initial screen appearance. She is a native of Bemidji, Minnesota.

(1948) JOAN CRAWFORD wore the outfit of a carnival dancing girl for her appearance at the Photographers' Costume Ball. Her brief attire is the same one she wore in the film *Flamingo Road*. Joan's dancing excellence started her on the road to film fame—her initial starring role in *Our Dancing Daughters* gaining her a long-term contract at MGM studios.

Let There Be Music

(1955)   JACK BENNY never missed an opportunity to perform as a violinist. Jack was a fine musician when he wasn't scratching out sour notes on his valuable Stradivarius as part of his amusing comedy routines. When he was a teenager, he was a member of an orchestra in Waukegan, Illinois, his hometown. He devoted considerable time and effort to fund raising for musical groups in many cities.

(1944) JOHN GARFIELD, one of the screen's most able portrayers of tough guys, much preferred to spend time in lighter activities, such as joining his daughter, Katharine, in song as she played her favorite tunes on the family piano. Born on New York City's Lower East Side, Garfield sold newspapers as a youngster. Participating in school debating contests helped him prepare for an acting career.

(1949) TONY MARTIN'S actress wife CYD CHARISSE, smiles her approval as the singer plays a tune on the clarinet, his favorite musical instrument. Tony was a member of swing bands before gaining fame as a vocalist. Cyd, too, has been closely associated with music since the age of eight, at which time she started ballet lessons in Amarillo, her Texas birthplace.

(1945) GARY COOPER learned the secret of horn-tooting from members of a junior orchestral group while waiting for a stage call at a holiday presentation in Hollywood. The lanky, Montana-born actor had plenty to toot about. Following college at Grinnel, Iowa, he came to Southern California seeking employment as a newspaper cartoonist. Instead, he switched to acting.

(1954) ROD CAMERON's severest musical critic was Bonzo, his pet
beagle, shown appraising the actor's ability with a guitar. One of the
screen's tallest leading men, the Canadian-born actor racked up
dozens of starring roles in action-filled movies. Rod was born in
Calgary. His family tree included several high government officials,
one of them, John MacInnes, Governor of Prince Edward Island.

(1955) OZZIE NELSON strums a banjo to the piano accompaniment of his wife, HARRIET, preparing for a musical sequence on one of their video programs. Their highly entertaining show, *The Adventures of Ozzie and Harriet,* brought happiness and laughs to countless millions of admirers for many years. America's youngest Eagle Scout at the age of thirteen, Ozzie also held a law degree from New Jersey Law School before switching to the world of entertainment. Jersey City was his birthplace. Harriet was born in Iowa.

(1944) MICKEY ROONEY doesn't kid around when he gets close to a set of drums—he's really good at beating out rhythm. The Brooklyn-born actor was introduced to theatergoers as an infant by his parents, vaudeville performers. Enacting the role of Mickey McGuire in a series of short subjects led him to forgo his real name, Joe Yule, Jr., and switch to the one he has since made famous throughout the world.

(1957) GENE KELLY is joined by the late NATALIE WOOD, beating out some rhythm as they blended their voices in song between takes of a film in which they shared acting honors. The petite, San Francisco-born actress started her acting career at the age of four. Kelly, a native of Pennsylvania and a graduate of the University of Pittsburgh, wears many hats—every one loaded with talent. World-famous as a dancer-actor, he also directs and is a highly capable choreographer.

(1948) BURT LANCASTER is the Piccolo Pete in this offstage photo
with YVONNE DECARLO, during a respite from the film in which she
was his leading lady. One of Hollywood's finest actors, with an Oscar
to prove it, Burt was a vaudeville and circus acrobat before being
introduced to moviegoers by the late Mark Hellinger, film producer
and popular newspaper columnist.

(1949) ELSA LANCHESTER was fortunate to have CHARLES LAUGHTON as a helpmate—as well as a husband. Shown assisting Elsa with some new vocal routines for her personal appearances, he often utilized his free time coaching other screen performers. Laughton was one of the screen's most capable dramatic actors, and his portrayal of Captain Bligh in *Mutiny on the Bounty* may never be equaled. Both he and his wife came to Hollywood from their native England.

(1955) DEAN MARTIN is unquestionably a highly talented singer
and actor. However, his horn-tooting ability evidently leaves some-
thing to be desired—judging from the reaction of his wife, JEANNIE.
A jack-of-all trades before seeking an acting career, Dean may be
the most prominent resident ever to emanate from Steubenville,
Ohio, his hometown.

(1947) ERROL FLYNN (*left*) and TOM D'ANDREA whiled away time playing harmonicas during free moments on the set of *Silver River*, a rip-roaring Western. World-famous for his swashbuckling screen performances, Flynn led an equally exciting life before seeking an acting career. He was born in Hobart, Tasmania, and educated in Paris and London, and his early occupations included boxing, pearl fishing and serving as cook on board a schooner. D'Andrea was both a writer and an actor.

Guys and Gals

(1958) JIMMY DURANTE never claimed he was beautiful—but will you look at that "fizz-zeek"! Referred to as "Schnozzola" by millions of his fans throughout the world, Durante was a famous landmark in the entertainment world since the early days of vaudeville. Starting as a piano pounder in 1912, he headlined every field of entertainment until illness sidelined him. To have known Jimmy was to love him.

(1947) MARILYN MONROE had not yet exploded onto motion-picture screens as a sex symbol when this photo was snapped. Note the brunette hair—her natural shade at eighteen. Her tragic death in 1962 cut short a career plagued with illness and heartbreak. Filmgoers throughout the world mourned her death—but none more so than her former husband, Joe DiMaggio.

(1953) GINGER ROGERS is a pleasant sight in her angora halter and short shorts posing at her hilltop home high above the film studios where she has starred in dozens of successful movies. Daily workouts on the tennis court are greatly responsible for the splendid figure displayed by this popular star. Like the late President of the United States, Harry S Truman, Ginger, too, has brought fame to Independence, Missouri, her birthplace.

(1956) JAYNE MANSFIELD and husband MICKEY HARGITAY. One of Hollywood's shapeliest blondes, the Bryn Mawr (Pennsylvania)-born actress lost her life in a tragic automobile accident in Louisiana at the age of thirty-three. Winner of numerous beauty contests, she was the favorite subject of photographers for several years—particularly in poses such as this with muscleman-weightlifter Mickey.

(1946) SUSAN HAYWARD created a major traffic jam while posing for this glamorous snapshot at the edge of the University of California at Los Angeles campus. Mother of twin sons, the shapely film star was a baseball addict during her childhood in Brooklyn, her birthplace. Magazine photos of her as a model brought her to the attention of film moguls. Susan won an Oscar in 1958 for her performance in *I Want to Live!*

(1948) ROBERT TAYLOR is an interested onlooker as AVA GARDNER
takes a soaking from property men preparing her for a closeup on
the set of *The Bribe*, in which she and Taylor shared acting honors.
Once the wife of Frank Sinatra, Ava has been living in Spain since
abandoning Hollywood. Few film queens possessed the eye-filling
figure of this North Carolinian.

(1946) JUNE HAVER soared to screen stardom with her curvaceous figure and perfect skin coloring—which made her an excellent subject for Technicolor films. Stage-struck from earliest childhood in Rock Island, Illinois, her birthplace, she was just six years old at the time of her stage debut in a little theater production. Later a screen talent scout discovered her singing with a band.

(1952) DIANA LYNN struck this provocative pose a split second
before the camera clicked. An excellent subject for photographers,
this native Californian also excelled as an actress, starting her screen
career in ingenue roles. In addition, her superior piano playing
brought her to the attention of film studios, and for a brief period
she was employed as a piano accompanist.

(1947) CARMEN MIRANDA uses an ordinary Turkish towel to form a head covering in the absence of one of her inimitable fruit-laden turbans. While many of her fans were under the impression that she was a native of Brazil, the fiery actress was actually born in Portugal. Star of numerous musical films, Carmen's real name would never have fit on a theater marquee—Maria do Carmo Miranda da Cunha.

(1947) JANET LEIGH was brand-new to Hollywood when this picture was made atop the roof of her home in Beverly Hills. Norma Shearer reportedly discovered Janet and was responsible for her being signed to a motion-picture contract. Her hometown friends in Merced, California, remember her as Jeanette Helen Morrison.

Stars and
Their Children

(1944) ANDY DEVINE and wife DOROTHY enjoyed each evening's prayer session with their two sons, TAD, nine (*left*) and five-year-old DENNY. Princess, their pet boxer—and inseparable pal—always shared the ritual with the boys. She, too, closed her eyes during the daily observance. An extra at the start of his acting career, Andy hailed from Arizona.

(1955) DEAN MARTIN and wife JEANNIE with two of their handsome sons. In Dean's arms is one-and-a-half-year-old RICCI. Peeking out from the lower right-hand corner is three-and-a-half-year-old DINO. A native Ohioan, Dean is one of the highest-paid entertainers in show business.

(1949) FRANK SINATRA and wife NANCY with their three lovely
children, five-year-old FRANK, JR., one-year-old CHRISTINA and
NANCY SANDRA, nine, seen in the garden of their spacious home in
Bel Air, adjacent to Beverly Hills. A successful audition with an
amateur group (Major Bowes') started Frank on his sensational rise
to international fame.

(1954)   JOAN CRAWFORD received corsages and much love from her adorable seven-year-old twin daughters, CATHY (*left*) and CYNTHIA. Envy of many of her motion-picture contemporaries for her outstanding screen attire, Joan for years was a stylesetter for well-dressed women throughout the world. San Antonio, Texas, claimed her for a native daughter.

(1954)   JANE POWELL had a wee bit of trouble convincing her one-and-a-half-year-old daughter, CISSIE, that the lion cub shown at right in this photo at the Clyde Beatty Circus would not harm her. Formerly wed to Geary Steffen, the actress became the bride of her escort, Pat Nerney, shortly after this date. A radio singer at age twelve, Jane was born in Portland, Oregon.

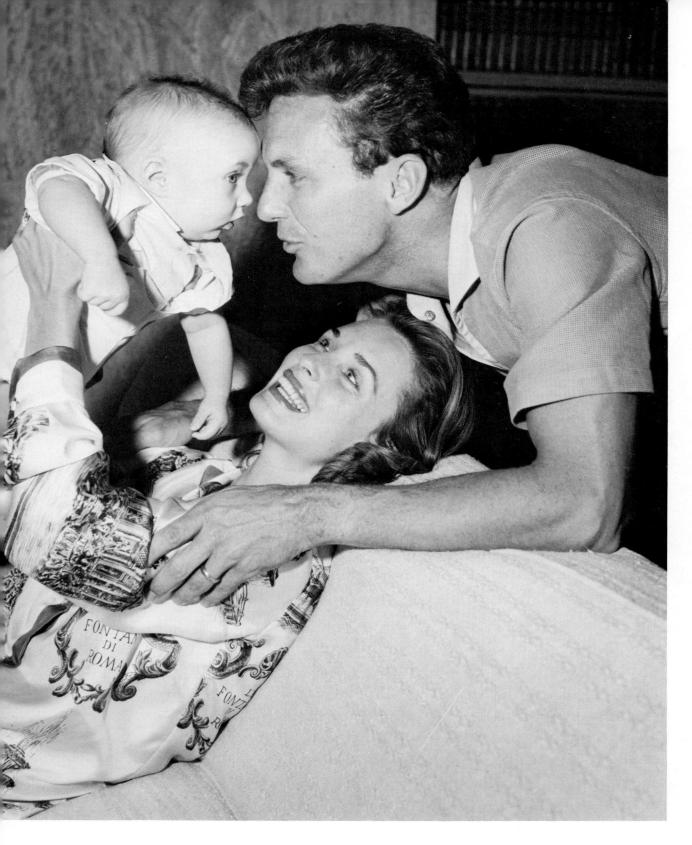

(1958) ROBERT STACK and his actress wife, ROSEMARIE BOWE, enjoy loving moments with their five-month-old son, CHARLES. Born in Los Angeles, Bob gained fame in television as well as in motion pictures. He headlined the dramatic TV series *The Untouchables* for many seasons. An excellent marksman, his favorite sport is skeet shooting.

(1948) BETTY HUTTON and her two-year-old daughter, LINDSAY (Briskin), practice the fine art of makeup. Born in Battle Creek, Michigan, Betty started her professional career as a singer. Her madcap comedy antics in films won her the title "Blonde Bombshell." She is also the mother of a younger daughter, equally as beautiful as Lindsay.

(1948) DANA ANDREWS took time out from his busy schedule to pacify the appetites of two of his children, five-year-old KATHY (*left*) and three-year-old STEPHEN. A native of Collins, Mississippi, educated at Sam Houston State College, Huntsville, Texas, Dana had planned a career as a certified public accountant before being spotted by a talent scout.

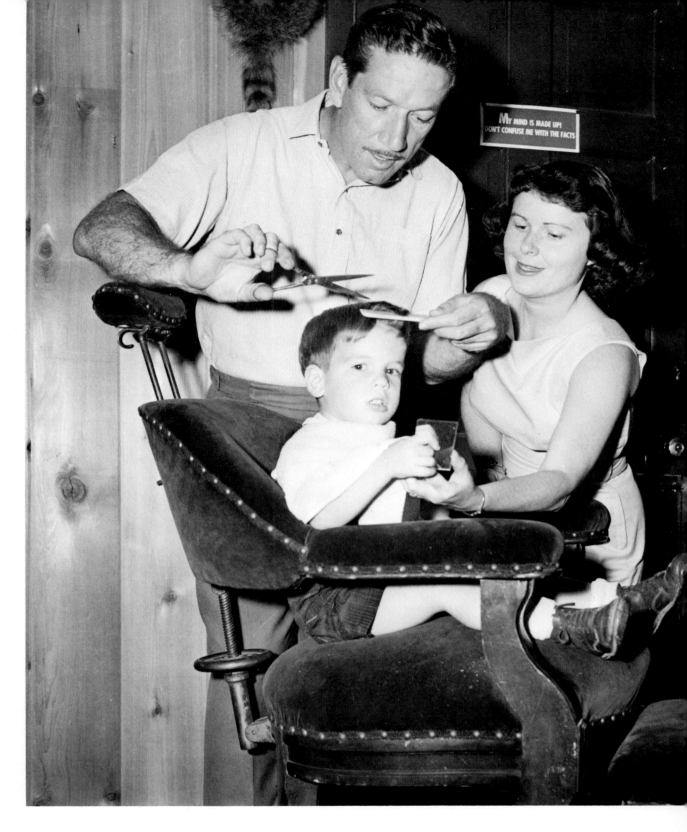

(1956) RICHARD BOONE was assisted by his wife, CLAIRE, as he trimmed the locks of their three-year-old son, PETER. The uphol-stered barber chair, a priceless antique, was once the property of Abraham Lincoln. Boone, who was born in Los Angeles, started his acting career as a drama student at Stanford University.

(1950) JOAN FONTAINE entertained her fifteen-month-old daughter, DEBORAH (Dozier), with multiple paper dolls cut from colored shelf paper. Unlike her daughter, a native of California, Joan was born in Tokyo of English parentage. She perfected her acting as a student of the famed Max Reinhardt, and won an Oscar in 1941 for her role in *Suspicion*.

(1950)   KIRK DOUGLAS purchased a toy electric shaver for his five-year-old son, MICHAEL, in order that the youngster might emulate his famous dad. Kirk's title role in the dramatic film *Champion* catapulted him to top stardom. He has also achieved success as a producer. Michael, too, has developed into a fine actor and is also a successful producer.

(1949)   EDDIE BRACKEN joined his children, MICHAEL and CAROLYN, in a game of ten pins—at their home in Brentwood. Only a little older than his children when he embarked upon an acting career, the Astoria (Long Island)-born comedy star was one of the original *Our Gang*-sters. The Professional Children's School for Actors in New York City helped Eddie prepare for his successful stage, screen and television roles.

(1957) JAMES MASON, his wife, PAMELA, and their eight-year-old daughter, PORTLAND, were interested spectators at a Hollywood party. Like Mason, his ex-wife and their daughter are also highly talented. The youngster aspired to follow in the footsteps of her famous dad. Pamela has combined acting with authoring books, writing a column for newspapers and hosting a late-night television talk show.

(1950) JACK CARSON and his eight-year-old son, JOHN, enjoyed happy times together at their ranch in the San Fernando Valley. Here the comedy star is teaching his son the fine art of whittling. The Canadian-born actor first donned greasepaint in amateur theatricals at Carleton College in Northfield, Minnesota.

(1950) GEORGE MONTGOMERY, DINAH SHORE and their three-year-old daughter, MISSY, were a happy family when this photograph was snapped at their ranch home in the San Fernando Valley. Although divorced, George and Dinah do share the love of a grandchild, presented to them recently by their now grown-up pride and joy. Along with being a fine actor, George is also the creator of handsome early-American-styled furniture—an example of which is visible in the background.

(1950) MARIO LANZA, his wife, BETTY, and their one-year-old daughter, COLLEEN, kept the entire neighborhood entertained with their vocalizing, a daily occurrence at their home in Beverly Hills. A piano mover in his native New York before being beckoned to Hollywood, Mario had a splendid voice, reminiscent of that of the great Enrico Caruso, which may be the best ever to be heard in motion pictures.

(1951) BRODERICK CRAWFORD started very early teaching his tiny son, KIM, the fundamentals of horseback riding. Like his famous daddy, the youngster enjoyed wearing Western attire. Winner of an Oscar for his performance in *All the King's Men*, Brod, too, stems from theatrical parents—Lester and Helen Broderick, the latter one of the most talented comediennes of stage and screen.

(1944) GEORGE MURPHY is the proud papa teaching the fine art of dancing to his two youngsters, DENNIS and MELISSE. George, a hoofer in a number of motion pictures, and his late wife, Julie, were a professional dance team before Hollywood beckoned to the Connecticut-born actor. New Haven was his birthplace on a Fourth of July. He is a graduate of Yale University, and the highlight of his life was serving as a United States Senator from California.

Terpsichore–
Hollywood Style

(1949) JOAN CRAWFORD and CESAR ROMERO were the life of the party as they set the pace for other dancers. One of Hollywood's best dancers, Romero has always been at the top of the list of party givers, much in demand as a dinner companion for the most glamorous women in town. Joan never failed to spend much of the evening dancing at social functions. While still a teenager she started collecting cups and prizes for her grace and ability.

(1956) JAMES CAGNEY and JANE GREER rehearse a soft-shoe dance routine during the filming of *Man of a Thousand Faces*. Multitalented Cagney enacted the title role—that of Lon Chaney, an early motion-picture great. A past president of the Screen Actors Guild, star of many of Hollywood's finest films, he was awarded an Oscar for his exceptional performance in *Yankee Doodle Dandy* in 1942. Jane, born in the nation's capital, Washington, D.C., was an orchestra singer at the time of her discovery for motion pictures.

(1957) The late NATALIE WOOD and husband ROBERT WAGNER make a handsome twosome dancing nose to nose at Ciro's. Youthful veterans of the screen, both started their acting careers at an early age. Bob, probably one of the best-looking leading men in Hollywood, is a popular star of television as well as motion pictures. Detroit is his hometown.

(1948)   DAVID NIVEN and wife HJORDIS dance away an evening at Club Mocambo. The Swedish beauty became the actor's bride after his former wife met her death in a tragic stairway fall. Usually seen as an Englishman in his screen appearances, Niven is Scottish, born in Kirriemuir. After graduating from Sandhurst, England's Royal Military Academy, he saw action with the Highland Light Infantry during World War II—wearing kilts, the customary uniform of his countrymen. His performance in *Separate Tables* won him an Oscar.

(1956) SHIRLEY MACLAINE and her producer husband, STEVE PARKER, dance cheek to cheek during a party at the Cocoanut Grove. Wed in 1954, Steve has spent a great part of his time in the Orient—while Shirley has divided her time between screen appearances, authoring books and involving herself in things political. Shirley is a brainy lady, well-liked by coworkers as well as film fans. A starring role on Broadway brought her to the attention of a Hollywood producer.

(1958)   CLARK GABLE and wife KAY joined other dancing couples at a dinner-dance following a film premiere. Gable was known as the "Romantic King" of motion pictures from 1930 on. No other actor even came close to challenging him for that title during his lengthy reign, ended only by his death in 1960. An actress at the time she wed Gable, Kay (Williams) gave up her career when she became the bride of the screen idol.

(1948) SPENCER TRACY and his wife, LOUISE, in a rare photograph—dancing at a Hollywood party. An actress at the time she met and wed Tracy, Louise (Treadwell) forsook her professional career to head up The Tracy Clinic, famous for the treatment of children, located in Los Angeles. Tracy, winner of two Oscars, left his home in Milwaukee, Wisconsin, to study acting at the American Academy of Dramatic Arts. Stage appearances led to Hollywood and immortality as one of the screen's finest actors.

(1954)   BOB HOPE dancing with his wife, DOLORES, during one of his brief periods at home. Probably the most-traveled personality of all time, particularly known for his visits with servicemen throughout the world, the veteran comedy star will one day have a museum to house the numberless awards and gifts showered upon him by organizations and nations for whom he has given his time and talent. The London-born star reached his seventy-fifth birthday in 1978.

(1951) FERNANDO LAMAS and LANA TURNER shared dance scenes as well as acting honors in *The Merry Widow*, a musical favorite in which the blond actress portrayed the provocative, wealthy widow. The dance sequences required many weeks of strenuous rehearsals— hard work, but great for Lana's super figure. Now directing as well as acting, the handsome Argentinian appeared in numerous films in his homeland before coming to Hollywood.

(1957)   SOPHIA LOREN and ANTHONY QUINN are a happy twosome at an after-theater party in Beverly Hills. Three Oscars, two of them Quinn's, attest to the acting excellence of this pair. Trained as a teacher before becoming an actress in her native Italy, Sophia is the wife of Carlo Ponti, leading Italian film producer. Born in Mexico, Quinn made his initial screen appearance as a child actor. During recent years he, too, has lived in Italy.

(1958) JACK LEMMON and actress wife FELICIA FARR enjoy an evening out at Romanoff's. A fine performer, winner of an Oscar, Jack made his acting debut at the age of four, following in the footsteps of his actor father. During World War II the Boston-born Lemmon went directly from Harvard University to the USS *Lake Champlain,* an aircraft carrier on which he served as communications officer.

(1944) ELEANOR POWELL made screen history as the dancing star of many of Hollywood's most entertaining musical films. Still a teenager when she lit up Broadway stages with her electrifying routines, the Massachusetts-born actress was named "The World's Greatest Feminine Tap Dancer" in 1934. *Born to Dance* was the title of one of her pictures—a most appropriate description of her. She became the mother of actor Peter Ford during her marriage to Glenn Ford, popular film leading man.

(1947) GREGORY PECK and his former wife, GRETA, during a night out at a Hollywood nightclub. Cheek-to-cheek dancing with his petite wife would have been impossible for this 6-foot, 2½-inch-tall screen star. Peck, born in La Jolla, California, is known for his fine screen performances. He received an Oscar for his role in *To Kill a Mockingbird* in 1962. Stage roles prepared him for his starring career in motion pictures.

(1946) REX HARRISON and actress wife LILLI PALMER joined other couples on the dance floor at Club Mocambo. Wed in 1943, the Austrian-born actress and the English-born actor costarred on the stage and in motion pictures. His convincing performance in the hit film *My Fair Lady* won him an Oscar, one of many acknowledgments of his versatility as a performer.

(1955) RICARDO MONTALBAN and wife GEORGIANA radiate their domestic bliss during an evening out at Club Mocambo. WALTER WINCHELL, well-known columnist, seen at left, may have been listening in on their happiness. Extremely proud of his Mexican heritage, Montalban devotes much of his time to functions that help increase better relations between his homeland and the United States. Younger sister of screen star Loretta Young, Georgiana preferred homemaking to an acting career.

(1944)   GEORGE TOBIAS, JOHN GARFIELD and WALTER BRENNAN (*left to right*) had fun during the filming of *Nobody Lives Forever*. This precision (?) dancing was not in the script, but it did afford an amusing moment for the trio of actors and resulted in an interesting photograph for their fans. Brennan, a three-time Academy Award winner, raised pineapples in Guatemala for four years after serving in France with the 26th Division during World War I. Born in Swampscott, Massachusetts, Brennan was educated as a technical engineer.

How About This One?

(1958) CARL SANDBURG (*left*) and MILTON BERLE in a facetious moment at a cocktail party hosted by the latter, honoring the brilliant Pulitzer Prize-winning poet and biographer. Amazingly spry at the age of eighty, Sandburg was in Hollywood for a personal appearance on one of Berle's television shows. The unusual gesture was Sandburg's way of greeting arriving guests.

(1956) DEAN MARTIN was in a happy mood as he duplicated the pose of a statue on the set of *Ten Thousand Bedrooms,* his initial starring role in a motion picture as a "single"—after years of sensational success teamed with comedian Jerry Lewis. Both Dean and Jerry proved they were highly capable of carrying out solo assignments—much to the surprise of some skeptics.

(1946)   HUMPHREY BOGART, famous for his screen tough guy roles, in an off-guard moment during an evening out. A fun-loving person in real life—unlike other stars of his caliber, he did not object to this photo, showing him with glasses perched on the end of his nose. An Oscar winner for his performance in *The African Queen* in 1951, Bogie rarely patronized nightclubs. He preferred to entertain friends at home.

(1946) JAMES CAGNEY (*left*) and FRANK MCHUGH were only clowning in this shot wherein they appeared to be involved in a dispute.
Two of Hollywood's nicest guys—as well as best friends—they were
putting on an act for the camera. Before retiring from the screen to
spend most of his time at his home in upstate New York, Cagney
enjoyed driving his racing sulky and trotting horses around the
quarter-mile track which adjoined his home in Beverly Hills.
McHugh, a native of Homestead, Pennsylvania, enacted numerous
comedy roles in films—always in convincing fashion.

(1949) MARLON BRANDO shares a wheelchair with costar TERESA WRIGHT on the set of *The Men*, his first film. His brilliant performance in the Broadway hit *A Streetcar Named Desire* left no doubt that Brando would also reach stardom in motion pictures. Born in Omaha, Nebraska, he originated a style of acting that has set a pattern for many aspiring actors. Hollywood voted him an Oscar for his dramatic performance in *On the Waterfront* in 1954.

(1946) WALLACE BEERY's lovely daughter, CAROL ANN, adjusts his black tie as the superstar of films evinced his displeasure at having to wear a dress suit at a Hollywood social affair. One of the screen's first box-office greats, born in Kansas City, Beery included among his earlier occupations, stints as chorus boy, elephant tender and riveter. No other actor has ever been capable of duplicating his inimitable acting style.

(1943) FRANK SINATRA displays his tonsils for MARTHA RAYE, fulfilling her request to see from whence comes his inimitable voice. A pair of clowns at heart, both gained top stardom as vocalists with a sound of their own. Awarded an honorary commission in the armed forces for her devotion to servicemen, whom she entertained constantly throughout the war years, the Montana-born songstress-comedienne brightened up many of Hollywood's most successful musical films with her wacky brand of acting.

(1951) MARGE and GOWER CHAMPION, for years the screen's most versatile dance team, were having a little offstage fun in this photograph—taken on the set of *Lovely to Look At,* a lavish musical in which they shared important scenes. Gower appeared to be attempting to get a closeup of Marge's molars. Gower became a topflight stage director and choreographer before his recent death. He served with the United States Coast Guard during World War II.

(1945) GROUCHO MARX, forever surrounded by screen beauties in his motion picture roles, is shown with RUTH ROMAN (*left*) and LISETTE VEREA on the set of *Adventures in Casablanca*, a Marx Brothers comedy. A talented musician—like his brothers Harpo and Chico—Groucho was considered one of the best guitar players in the country. For years one of television's topmost attractions, he also wrote entertaining books.

(1946) FRANK MORGAN (*left*) chose EDWARD G. ROBINSON for a dancing partner at a Hollywood party—and proceeded to demonstrate some new Latin dances. Morgan, white-haired comedy star of many motion pictures, was always good for a laugh and a welcome guest at every Hollywood soiree. Robinson, the screen's number one tough guy, also enjoyed the Hollywood social set. Had he not been typed as a heavy, he probably would have gained equal fame as a comedian.

(1946)   RED SKELTON's late wife, GEORGIA, stands by as the beloved comedian has some fun with a checkroom cutie at Ciro's. Red is offering the girl her choice of the contents of either hand as a tip; one hand held a normal gratuity, the other, a much larger sum. From a humble start in medicine shows and showboats, Red climbed to the top of the ladder in show business, following in the footsteps of his father, Joseph Skelton, one of the renowned circus clowns of the Gay Nineties.

(1946)   ARTHUR TREACHER wraps MARGARET O'BRIEN in his camel's hair coat to shield the petite actress from the cold breezes during a performance of the Ice Capades in Hollywood. Famous for his screen portrayals of butlers, British-born Treacher was a musical comedy stage star before motion pictures typed him as the most highly paid and best-known butler in the world.

(1945) JOE E. BROWN is saying, "Don't fence me in," as he tries to go past CHARLES RUGGLES during an intermission period at a Hollywood theater. Veterans of stage and screen and longtime friends, Joe and Charlie could always be depended upon to lend a touch of comedy to stills as well as to motion pictures. Born in Los Angeles, Ruggles started his acting career at the age of fifteen in San Francisco.

(1947) WILLIAM POWELL and his wife, DIANA, share a woolen blanket while sitting ringside at a performance of the *Ice Follies*. It helped ward off showers of flying ice as well as cold breezes. An acting career studded with many great performances might never have materialized for Bill if he had complied with the desire of his parents and become an attorney. The Pittsburgh-born actor's studies at the American Academy of Dramatic Arts started him on an acting career.

(1953) MARILYN MONROE and DANNY THOMAS share a friendly clinch between curtain calls of a benefit show at Shrine Auditorium in Los Angeles. Number one glamour queen of the screen at the time of her death in 1962, Marilyn carved a niche for herself in motion pictures that has never been filled. Many other film beauties have tried—unsuccessfully. Her popularity bore out the fact that *Gentlemen Prefer Blondes,* one of her motion pictures.

(1945) EDDIE CANTOR, DANNY KAYE and GEORGE BURNS (*from left to right*), a comedy trio par excellence, engaged in this kissing bee at a cocktail party hosted by Cantor, honoring Danny upon the start of the latter's new radio show. Aside from their mutual affection for each other—and the fact that the three of them attained stardom on stage, screen, radio and television—they also hailed from the same state, New York.

Hugs and Kisses

(1950) JUDY GARLAND and daughter LIZA MINNELLI share this affectionate moment just as the talented tot was about to go onstage in her "chick" outfit to enact a leading role in an Easter Day program. Today one of the entertainment world's most popular stars, Liza is doing an excellent job following in the footsteps of her late, beloved mother. Her father, Vincente Minnelli, is a top film director.

(1956) LANA TURNER and JERRY LEWIS smooch as they greet each other at a social gathering in Hollywood. World-famous for his zany comedy routines in every branch of show business, Jerry is also an excellent writer, director and producer. He typifies the proverbial one-man show. A great deal of his time is devoted now to raising funds for medical research.

(1953) DEBBIE REYNOLDS (*left*) and TERRY MOORE offer JOHN WAYNE their affectionate congratulations at an after-theater party following the premiere showing of his motion picture, *Island in the Sky*. Awarded an Oscar for his convincing performance in *True Grit*, Wayne in real life courageously continued his acting career despite serious medical setbacks.

(1945) ALAN LADD's daughter, ALANA, was his favorite leading lady, even at the age of twenty months, envied by countless millions of other beauties, who would have loved to share a "bussing" session with the Arkansas-born film star. A diving champion before seeking a screen career, Ladd made his initial appearance on a motion-picture sound stage as a grip, akin to a carpenter. Born in Hot Springs, he won athletic honors as a student at North Hollywood High School.

(1948) LIONEL BARRYMORE received a warm thanks from CLAIRE TREVOR for giving her moral support from the sidelines as she performed for the sound camera in a scene from *Key Largo*. Hollywood voted her an Oscar for her performance in that dramatic film. Her studies at the American Academy of Dramatic Arts in her native New York, and subsequent stage roles on Broadway, won Claire a motion-picture contract.

(1954) VIRGINIA GREY got a bear hug from ANDY DEVINE on her
arrival at a barn dance hosted by the beloved actor. A native of
Southern California, the daughter of a pioneer film director,
Virginia made her screen debut at the age of nine as Little Eva, in
Uncle Tom's Cabin. Andy was possibly Hollywood's largest actor,
whose gravel voice was his trademark in dozens of motion pictures
and on television.

(1956) JAMES CAGNEY and BARBARA STANWYCK—two of the screen's greatest stars and friends for many years—were happy to be costarred in the film *Somewhere I'll Find Him*. A pair of native New Yorkers, both started their professional careers in musical presentations, later gaining worldwide fame enacting some of the screen's most difficult dramatic roles. All of Hollywood displayed their admiration for Cagney at an industry tribute on his seventy-fifth birthday.

(1958) MIYOSHI UMEKI and RED BUTTONS—winners of Oscars for their costarring husband-and-wife roles in *Sayonara*—congratulated each other while clinging to their awards following the presentations in Hollywood. Best known as a comedian, Red, like many other top comics, started in burlesque (Minsky's) en route to the stage, television and motion pictures. Now a happy Californian, he was born in New York.

(1955) SONJA HENIE had a warm greeting for LIBERACE, a guest at a costume party she hosted at her Hollywood home. Two of the world's most popular entertainers, both achieved top stardom in their respective fields of endeavor. Unequaled as an ice-skating champion from earliest childhood, Sonja filled her home to over-flowing with trophies. She also collected the works of many renowned artists. Liberace also collects—homes, pianos and money.

(1945)   REGINALD GARDINER kisses GREER GARSON on her arrival at
a Russian Easter party hosted by the actor and his Russian-born
wife, Nadia. It is traditional at holiday-time for Russians to embrace
and kiss three times. Although Reggie is a native of England, need it
be said that he had a most enjoyable evening—kissing many film
beauties like Greer. Londoners remember him as a successful stage
actor prior to his departure for Hollywood screen roles.

(1949) DOROTHY LAMOUR (*left*) receives a friendly greeting from
BETTY HUTTON at a social gathering. Always one of the screen's
best-dressed stars, Dotty sports a new chapeau—topped off by white
egret feathers. Betty, too, was a stylesetter in real life.

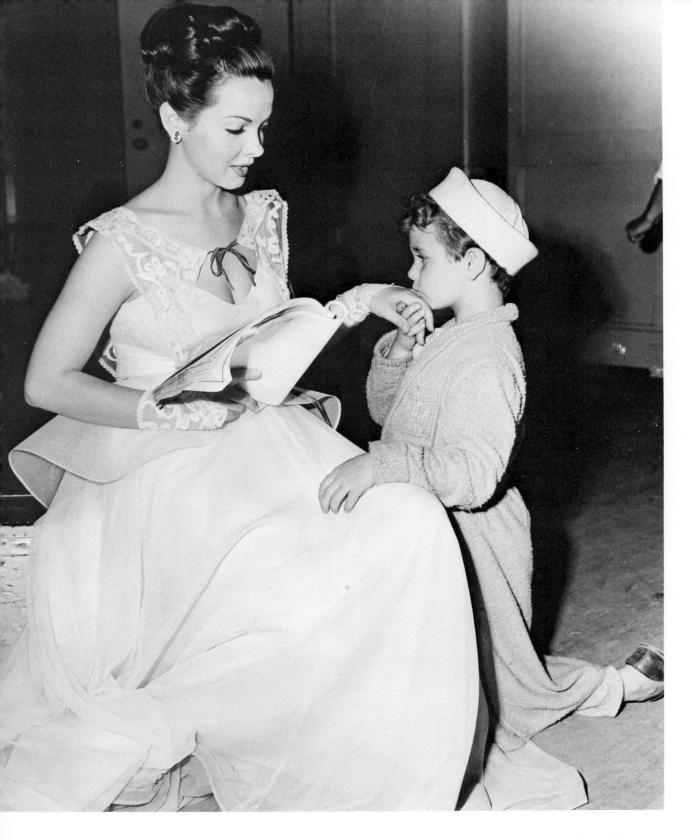

(1944) KATHRYN GRAYSON and DEAN STOCKWELL share this romantic scene during a rest period on the set of *Anchors Aweigh*. The
seven-year-old actor suggested that a good pose might be to show
him proposing to the motion-picture songstress. She agreed with
him and the talented youngster proceeded to display his charm.
Dean was one of the few child actors to continue to adult roles in
films.

(1952) LAUREN BACALL and GEORGE JESSEL share this friendly
greeting at a cocktail party at Chasen's. Happily wed to Humphrey
Bogart for a dozen years until his death in 1957, the actress is a
native New Yorker, known to her many friends as Betty, her real
name. Jessel, a veteran entertainer of every branch of show
business, also gained fame as the master of ceremonies of countless
social functions, thereby living up to the title bestowed upon him—
"Toastmaster General."

(1946) LUCILLE BALL and DESI ARNAZ managed this quick kiss when a friend conveniently danced the red-haired comedienne up to the bandstand at Ciro's, where the multitalented Cuban was conducting the orchestra. Although their marriage fizzled, their Desilu-produced television shows were among the most popular ever offered TV fans—and will continue to be shown to new audiences for years to come. Both became multimillionaires when they sold their production company.

(1948)   LORETTA YOUNG (*left*) and ROSALIND RUSSELL display their
friendship for each other with this embrace at a dinner party
following the former's acceptance of an Oscar for her performance
in *The Farmer's Daughter*. The hug was obviously enthusiastic even
though Roz was also one of the nominees for the coveted trophy
that year. One of the bravest as well as finest actresses in motion
pictures, Roz fought courageously to overcome a terminal illness
which took her life a short time ago.

(1954) JIMMY DURANTE plants a birthday kiss on TALLULAH BANK-
HEAD's cheek at a dinner party honoring the prominent stage and
screen actress. Tallulah was born in Huntsville, Alabama, into a
politically famous family—her father was William Bankhead,
Speaker of the House of Representatives. Her victory in a beauty
contest at the age of sixteen started her on her professional career.
Following this kiss, Durante remarked, "Kinda dreamy, ain't it?"

Stars and Pets

(1950) JANET BLAIR's pet pooch, Max, liked to get his nose into the act when the glamorous screen and stage star rehearsed vocal numbers for personal-appearance engagements. Footlight trouping brought Janet to the attention of Hollywood producers. A favorite with Broadway theatergoers, Janet was born in Blair, Pennsylvania.

(1956)   EDDIE FISHER appeared to approve DEBBIE REYNOLD's love-making with their pet poodle, Rocky. They're posing on the set of *Bundle of Joy,* a romantic musical in which they both appeared—and which marked Eddie's debut as a screen actor. Their first child was due to arrive just two months after this photograph was taken. Philadelphia claims Eddie for a native son.

(1956) RONALD REAGAN and actress wife NANCY DAVIS share a moment with their pet collie, Lucky, in the garden of their Pacific Palisades home, a short distance from the blue Pacific. A highly versatile performer throughout his acting career, Ronnie's screen roles ran the gamut from slapstick comedy to stark drama.

(1944)   WILLIAM BENDIX displays a look of envy as his wife, TESS, serves lunch to their pet, Riley, in the latter's domicile in their garden. Born on New York's East Side, Bill had early aspirations toward a baseball career—serving briefly as a batboy for the New York Giants. Dissuaded by his parents from furthering that ambition, he turned to dramatics—starting with New York Theater Guild plays. Spotted by a film talent scout, the husky actor was an immediate success in Hollywood.

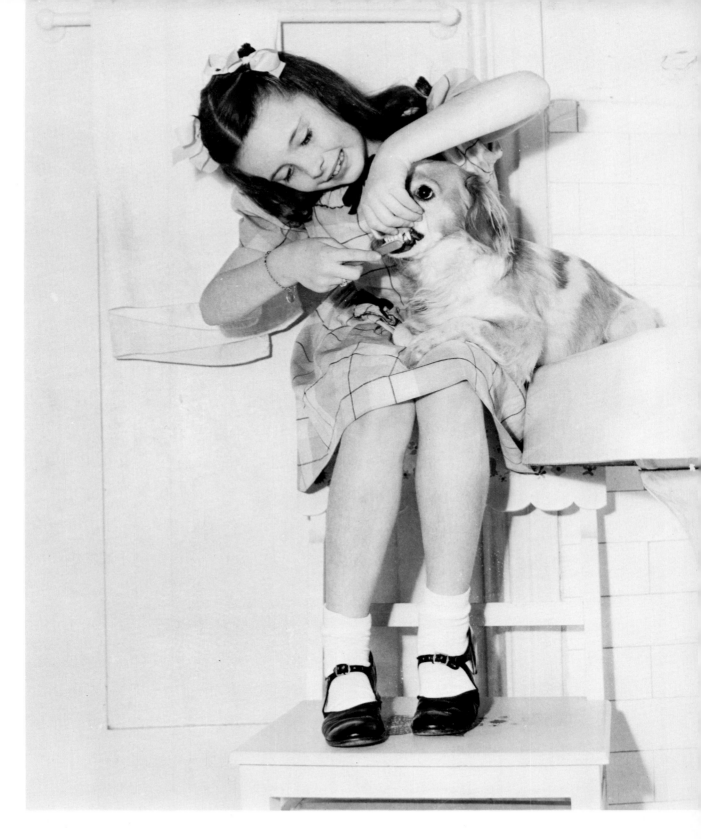

(1945) MARGARET O'BRIEN insisted upon brushing the teeth of her pet cocker spaniel, Maggie, before permitting photographs to be taken. Eight years old at the time of this pose, the brilliant young actress was already the recipient of a miniature Oscar for her excellent acting. Born in Los Angeles, she started acting at the age of four—and in a short time she became one of the screen's top box-office attractions.

(1950) DONALD O'CONNOR and wife GWEN were the recipients of puppy love as they fed the new, roly-poly members of their household. Don, too, was just a "pup" when he joined the family act in vaudeville, later becoming one of the screen's leading dance and comedy stars. Gwen (Carter) shared stage appearances with Don during their marriage. Chicago is his hometown.

(1949) CESAR ROMERO was joined by HOLLY HOPE, his five-year-old niece, in teaching new tricks to his pet Boston bull, Squeak, at the actor's home in Brentwood. A popular screen actor since coming to Hollywood from Broadway in the early 1930s, the perennial bachelor has appeared in a large variety of motion pictures—at the same time headlining hit television shows. Of Latin parentage, he was born in New York.

(1949) ARLENE DAHL and her pet parakeet are certainly birds of a feather. Both are beautiful—and easy to listen to when they chirp, each in her own way. Named "Most Likely to Succeed" by her classmates in high school, the Minneapolis-born beauty has lived up to that prediction. One of the highest-paid professional models before making her screen debut, she looks equally well in swimsuits or evening gowns.

(1943) SHIRLEY TEMPLE is joined by her pet Pekingese in this happy scene at her Hollywood home. An actress from the time she was just three years old, the curly-topped star of numerous hit pictures was born in Santa Monica and (believe it or not) celebrated her fiftieth birthday in 1979.

(1949) RHONDA FLEMING's pet Dalmation, Thumper, must have been the envy of the entire canine world—sharing a home with the beautiful, titian-haired actress. While Rhonda is among the many film personalities who were born in Southern California, she is one of only a handful to gain top-rank stardom in motion pictures. Stage performances brought her to the attention of Hollywood producers.

(1944) ALICE FAYE kept a close watch as two-year-old ALICE, JR., fed tidbits to their Belgian shepherd, Wonga. Wife of bandleader-comedian Phil Harris, the blond star of many top musical films is also the mother of another daughter, Phyllis. At the height of her screen career she elected to retire from acting to devote all of her time to homemaking and motherhood. Alice was a singer with Rudy Vallee's orchestra before embarking upon the road to motion-picture fame.

Behind the Scenes

(1956) ELIZABETH TAYLOR gave her hair a last-minute check before facing cameras on the set of *Raintree County*, a $5,000,000 production, MGM's biggest budget at the time for a domestic production. Like Vivien Leigh in *Gone With the Wind*, Elizabeth played a Southern belle in a gripping love story of America during the war between the states. The British-born actress was already the mother of two sons.

(1945) BETTY GRABLE (*left*) and JUNE HAVER made up to look alike for the hit film *The Dolly Sisters*. For years Betty reigned as Hollywood's pinup queen, and rightly so. GIs fortunate enough to have one of her glamorous photos in their lockers knew her contours better than they knew their own rifles. June, at thirteen, was a vocal soloist with a prominent orchestra in her Illinois hometown.

(1946) VIVIAN BLAINE was an observer as GEORGE MONTGOMERY was fitted for a moustache on the set of *Three Little Girls in Blue*, a film in which they shared scenes. Moustaches of every description are kept handy by studio makeup artists, making it unnecessary for actors to grow their own lip adornments. This was George's first film upon returning to Hollywood after serving in the United States Army.

(1956)   LORETTA YOUNG's hairdresser made certain every hair was in place before the star of screen and television faced the movie camera. Her unlimited talent in motion-picture roles carried over into TV, where she produced as well as headlined her own hit program, *The Loretta Young Show*. A teenager at the time of her acting debut, her hometown friends in Salt Lake City knew her as Gretchen, her real name.

(1958) CLAUDE RAINS preferred to trim his own moustache during the filming of *This Earth Is Mine*, a dramatic picture in which the London-born actor appeared as an Alsatian winemaker. Once a call boy at His Majesty's Theatre in his native city, he was also a tutor at the Royal Academy of Dramatic Art. Stage and screen roles brought him international fame.

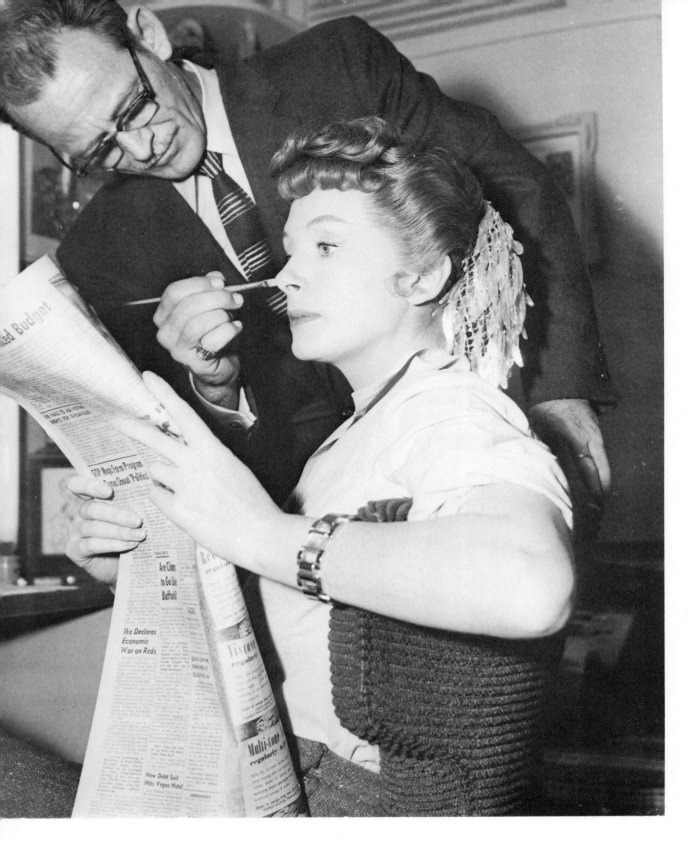

(1956) DEBORAH KERR used makeup periods to keep up with the latest news between scenes on the set of *The King and I*, one of her most popular screen vehicles. Deborah, who was born in Helensburgh, Scotland, went on to stage and screen successes in England. These led to her importation to Hollywood. She received critical as well as public acclaim for her outstanding performance in *Tea and Sympathy*—on Broadway and on the screen.

(1948) PATRICIA NEAL had the expert assistance of veteran actor EDWARD ARNOLD as she prepared for her initial screen appearance in *John Loves Mary*. Hollywood discovered the actress on Broadway, where she attracted considerable attention in the hit show *Another Part of the Forest*. In 1964 Hollywood honored the Kentucky-born actress with an Oscar for her admirable performance in *Hud*.

(1946) MERLE OBERON (*left*) and veteran stage and screen star
LENORE ULRIC shared this closeup during a brief production lull on
the set of *Bella Donna*, in which they also shared acting honors. Miss
Ulric came out of retirement for this film role. Oldtimers may
remember her as the star in the hit stage plays *Kiki* and *Lulu Belle*.

(1946)   CARY GRANT filled in for an absentee hairdresser as INGRID BERGMAN adjusted her hairdo for their next scene in *Notorious*, a classic film in which the Stockholm-born actress was afforded an opportunity to be her most glamorous. Winner of an Oscar in 1944 for *Gaslight*, Ingrid added another of the coveted trophies to her collection in 1956 for her brilliant work in *Anastasia*.

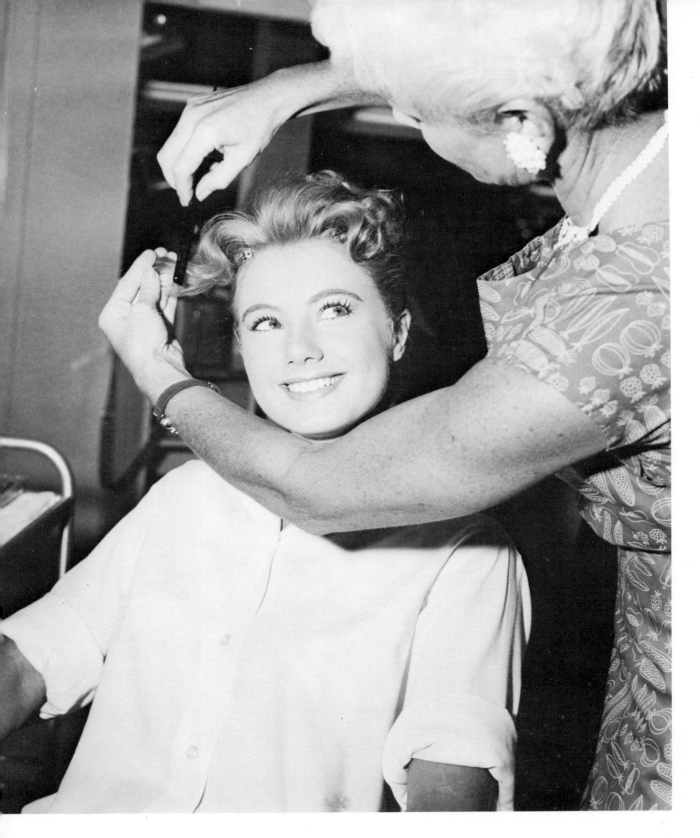

(1957) SHIRLEY JONES, encircled by the arms of an expert hair stylist, seems pleased with the attention being given her hair for her costarring role with Pat Boone in *April Love*. Winner of numerous acting and singing honors starting with her school days in Smithton, Pennsylvania, Shirley was rewarded with an Oscar in 1960 for her performance in *Elmer Gantry*. Singer David Cassidy is one of her talented sons.

(1951) GENE KELLY gladly assists LESLIE CARON with her makeup in preparation for her American film debut with him in *An American in Paris*. Just nineteen at the time, the talented French mademoiselle was a ballerina with the Ballets des Champs-Elysées in Paris when Kelly discovered and film-tested her for the leading role opposite him in the resulting box-office success. Her exceptional performance in this film endeared her to moviegoers everywhere.

Stellar Pastimes

(1949) CLARK GABLE was a familiar figure along the highways of Southern California astride his fast-moving motorcycle—until he wed Lady Sylvia Ashley. His bride, some close friends and studio heads all convinced the screen idol that the pastime was far too dangerous for a man with his responsibilities. The handsome star loved fast motors and screen roles that included action-filled sequences. His final film, *The Misfits,* in which he costarred with Marilyn Monroe, was one of his most rugged.

(1949) TYRONE POWER and his actress wife, LINDA CHRISTIAN, were avid camera enthusiasts. The footage shot by them during lengthy overseas junkets was sufficient to make up a fabulous, full-length motion picture. Editing the exposed film was a favorite pastime for the actor between assignments. His untimely death occurred in Spain during the filming of his final picture, *Solomon and Sheba*. Born in Cincinnati, Ty served with the United States Marine Corps during World War II.

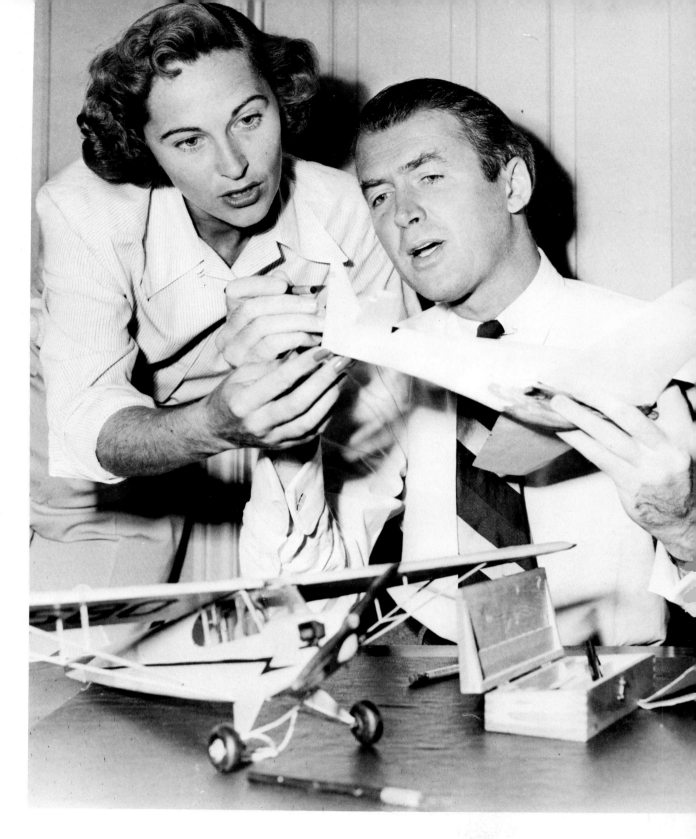

(1949) JAMES STEWART and his wife, GLORIA, enjoyed a mutual hobby, building miniature airplanes. An aviation buff since childhood, the lanky film star also enjoyed flying every kind of airplane. He was one of the first screen notables to don a uniform in World War II. His loyalty and all-out effort as a member of the Air Force won him millions of additional admirers—plus a gold star. His fine acting has also resulted in top awards, including an Oscar.

(1954) GILBERT ROLAND, one of Hollywood's best tennis players, made a habit of leaping over the net each time he defeated an opponent. Had he so desired, the handsome leading man might easily have become a top tennis star. As a youth in his native Mexico—Chihuahua, to be exact—he deliberated following in the footsteps of his father, Francisco Alonso, a much-admired Spanish bullfighter. With his family, Roland moved to Texas when Pancho Villa ordered the Spaniards out of Mexico.

(1951) ROBERT WALKER admires the handiwork of HELEN HAYES between takes on the set of *My Son John,* a dramatic film in which the veteran actress portrayed the late actor's mother. Her needlework, like her acting, has always been of the finest quality. Widow of the late Charles MacArthur, well-known playwright and screenwriter, she is the proud mother of James MacArthur, a fine actor. Her many honors include two Oscars.

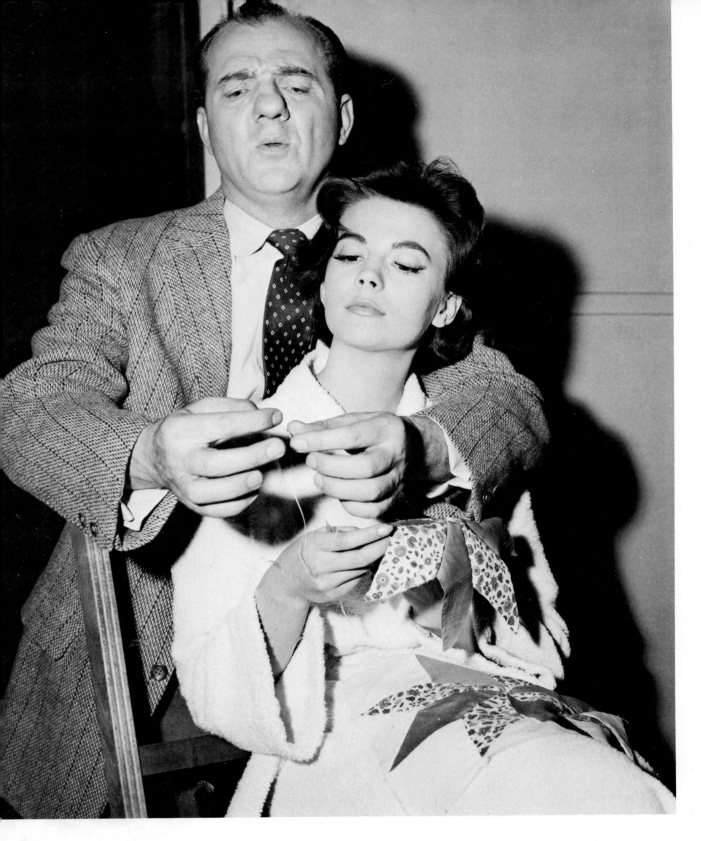

(1957) KARL MALDEN offers the late NATALIE WOOD his assistance in threading a needle—in order that the lovely actress can continue sewing squares for a crazy quilt between scenes of their costarring film, *Bombers B-52*. Winner of an Oscar in 1951 for his fine performance in *A Streetcar Named Desire*, Malden was born in Gary, Indiana, of Yugoslavian descent. His real name is Malden Sekulovich.

(1949) JUNE ALLYSON and DICK POWELL were two of Hollywood's most enthusiastic fishermen. The actor-producer's annual vacation never failed to include a try for some of the big fish off the coast of Southern California, generally from the deck of his luxurious yacht. Born in Mountain View, Arkansas, Dick started his professional career as a musician, then sang his way to fame in every branch of show business.

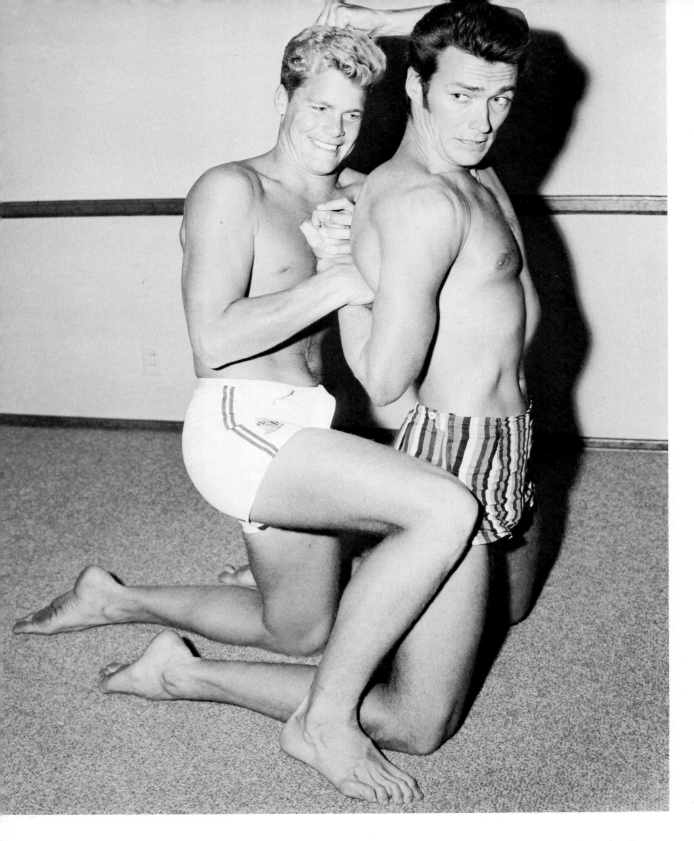

(1958) DOUG MCCLURE (*left*) and CLINT EASTWOOD, a pair of screen and television favorites, weren't kidding when they got together for occasional workouts—especially wrestling. Someone should have warned Clint that hairpulling is illegal. The handsome Californian's athletic prowess has stood him in good stead in the dramatic, two-fisted roles for which he has gained worldwide fame.

(1946)   PETER LAWFORD (*left*) joins JACKIE (BUTCH) JENKINS in a session of mumblety-peg, a traditional boy's game wherein the players use jackknives and try to outdo each other in finding new ways to toss them. The freckle-faced youngster won the game when he propped his knife on his nose and made a fancy throw. Pete decided not to attempt that one. They shared acting honors in *My Brother Talks to Horses*, an amusing film in which Jackie enacted the lead role.

(1948) FARLEY GRANGER and GERALDINE BROOKS shared a mutual hobby, archery, causing their friends to wonder if one of Dan Cupid's missiles might have chosen them as a target. California-born Farley attended Hollywood High School before making his motion-picture debut in a Samuel Goldwyn production. Gerry, one of the screen's most accomplished performers, belongs to a famous clothes-manufacturing clan—Stroock, which is her real last name.

(1958) ROBERT CUMMINGS looked like someone from another planet as he gazed through a magnifying glass while working on a ship model. His wife, MARY, joined the actor in his favorite pastime. Turning to television after scoring numerous successes in motion pictures, Bob became one of the small screen's most popular stars— portraying a bachelor photographer in *The Bob Cummings Show*. Born in Joplin, Missouri, educated at Carnegie Tech., he appeared in Broadway musicals before coming to Hollywood.

(1953) EDWARD G. ROBINSON and his wife, GLADYS, shared an artistic talent, painting. Daughter of a sculptor, Mrs. Robinson practiced her art in every corner of the world—specializing in oil painting. Eddie was one of the world's leading connoisseurs, during his lifetime collecting many great works of art. He built a complete museum on the grounds of his home in Beverly Hills to house his collection.

Some Diet–
Some Don't

(1944) BUD ABBOTT (*bottom*) and LOU COSTELLO hosted MARILYN
MAXWELL to a spaghetti lunch—prepared by Lou in his dressing-
room trailer on the set of *Lost in a Harem,* one of the comedy duo's
many hilarious comedies. As funny off the screen as on, Bud and
Lou rarely ever studied their scripts. A couple of minutes of
rehearsal before each take, and the pair were ready to shoot the
scene. Born in New Jersey of Italian parentage, Costello was
christened Louis Francis Cristillo.

(1949) ELIZABETH TAYLOR's mother, SARA, started teaching the beautiful young film star the fine art of cooking when the latter was still a teenager, as shown here at their home in Beverly Hills. Mrs. Taylor also was an actress (Sara Sothern) before joining her husband in his art gallery. They brought their talented daughter to Southern California from their native England when World War II was imminent.

(1956) JERRY COLONNA's wife, FLORENCE, piles his plate high with
his favorite food, spaghetti, during a luncheon in Las Vegas, where
they were attending the premiere showing of his latest film, *Meet Me
in Las Vegas*. Bulging eyes and a walrus moustache were trademarks
for Jerry, a talented comedian-singer-musician. He shared acting
honors with Bob Hope and Bing Crosby in a number of their Road
pictures.

(1945) JIMMY DURANTE exclaimed, "What's wit da pinkie?" when JOAN BLONDELL suggested that he keep his little finger well up when pouring tea into his cup. The blond actress hosted daily tea parties during the filming of *Strange Adventure*, serving goodies from her home each afternoon at four o'clock. Born in New York, daughter of professional actors, Joan made her stage debut when only a few months old.

(1946) RONALD REAGAN and his former wife, JANE WYMAN, couldn't resist sampling the smoked Italian ham, a specialty of Restaurant LaRue. Both stars in their own right at the time of their first meeting, they fell in love during the filming of a picture in which they were teamed romantically. Jane, a versatile actress born in St. Joseph, Missouri, gave an outstanding performance in *Johnny Belinda* in 1948, which won her an Oscar.

(1946) KEENAN WYNN (*left*) and PETER LAWFORD are the musclemen attacking a giant Swiss cheese at this party. Schooners of beer helped the clowning actors wash down their dairy loot. Close friends from the inception of their Hollywood careers, each donned greasepaint at a very early age. Keenan followed in the footsteps of his famous dad, Ed Wynn, one of the most brilliant comedy stars of all time.

(1956) GEORGE BURNS and his wife, GRACIE ALLEN, dug into the
lavish buffet at a cocktail party honoring Walter Winchell. Comedy
partners even before their marriage in 1925, George and Gracie
could have written a book on how to be happily married—while
sharing acting and billing honors. Her death brought sadness to
millions of fans who admired the San Francisco-born comedienne
over a long period of time.

(1946)   GLORIA DEHAVEN shocked JOHN PAYNE, her former husband, when she actually served him a portion of salad—in his ten-
gallon hat—while attending a Western costume ball in Hollywood.
A Virginian by birth, the popular actor was very gallant about this
unique service. A native of Los Angeles, daughter of theatrical
parents, Gloria was one of the screen's tiniest—and shapeliest—
beauties.

(1955) CHARLTON HESTON and his actress wife, LYDIA CLARKE, select tasty tidbits of food in this party photo. Awarded an Oscar for his fine performance in *Ben Hur* in 1959, the Illinois-born star, much in demand by film producers, actually worked in two films at the same time in order to fulfill lucrative commitments. Many of his screen roles required lavish costumes, entailing endless hours of preparation before facing movie cameras each day.

(1945)   DON AMECHE and CLAUDETTE COLBERT may have destroyed an old tradition when they substituted milk for coffee with doughnuts while sharing romantic scenes in *Guest Wife*. They also co-starred in an earlier hit film, *Midnight*. Educated at the University of Wisconsin, in his home state, Ameche brightened many entertaining musical films—sharing acting honors with Hollywood's most beautiful women.

(1944) JOSEPH COTTEN and JENNIFER JONES indulged in America's favorite repast, hot dogs—with mustard—during a break in the filming of *Love Letters*. Years of stage appearances preceded Joe's film debut in *Citizen Kane* in 1941. He is a southerner born in Petersburg, Virginia, and most of his film assignments have been highly dramatic—well-acted in every instance.

(1956)   FRED MACMURRAY and his actress wife, JUNE HAVER, were the envy of their Hollywood cohorts, since they were able to eat any and everything without adding ungainly weight. Fred's daily rounds of golf probably accounted for his ability to maintain his proper measurements. As for June, her figure always added up to perfection. The screen lost one of its most popular beauties when she switched from filmmaking to homemaking.

(1944)   VICTOR MOORE and EVELYN KEYES share a soft drink during
a brief spell from filmmaking on a warm day in Hollywood. The
actress admitted that she was being especially nice to the veteran
comedy star—because she had hopes of making a deal for his
Hollywood home when he departed for a role in a Broadway show.

Happy Hollywood

(1947) AL JOLSON and his wife, ERLE, had good reason to light up Hollywood Park racetrack with those big smiles. Jolson had the winner in a just-completed race—at seventeen-to-one odds. Legendary singing star of vaudeville, stage and screen, Jolson was one of the first entertainers to appear in talking pictures, amazing moviegoers with his vocalizing in the 1927 film *The Jazz Singer*. Born in St. Petersburg, Russia, Joley was brought by his parents to the United States as a youth.

(1948)   FRANK SINATRA (*left*) and EDDIE FISHER were among a host
of notables at an awards dinner in Hollywood. Both started their
vocal careers as band singers. Frank is a native of New Jersey. Fisher
was born in Philadelphia.

(1954)   ROBERT MITCHUM and his wife, DOROTHY, were among the happy guests at a Hollywood coctail party. Wed in 1940, they have two sons who are also actors. Bob, a GI during World War II, had the starring role in *The Story of G.I. Joe,* which catapulted him to top-bracket importance in motion pictures. The Connecticut-born star made his film acting debut in a Hopalong Cassidy film.

(1947) ROBERT TAYLOR and actress wife BARBARA STANWYCK pictured during happier days—spending an evening at Ciro's. Blessed with a perfect complexion, Barbara wore little, if any, makeup for many of her screen roles. Even freckles added to her glamour. She changed her name upon arriving in Hollywood: Her hometown friends in Brooklyn remember her as Ruby Stevens.

(1950) RED SKELTON (*left*) and FRED ASTAIRE are enjoying the former's hilarious jokes during a break in production on the set of *Three Little Words*, a musical film in which they costarred. Born in Omaha, Nebraska, Fred once teamed with his sister, Adele, as dancing vaudevillians.

(1953)   PAUL DOUGLAS was amused by his actress wife, JAN STER-
LING, as she resorted to gestures to point up a story she is relating
during dinner at Romanoff's. Paul was one of the stage and screen's
better actors, and his death in 1959 shocked his many friends and
fans. Educated at Yale University, he was a radio announcer-
commentator before becoming an actor.

(1944) ORSON WELLES and wife RITA HAYWORTH had good reason to exude happiness as they dined at Restaurant LaRue. The red-haired actress was expecting to become a mother in just a few months. Often referred to as the "Wonder Boy" of the entertainment world, Welles, a native of Kenosha, Wisconsin, proved worthy of that accolade—gaining honors as a writer, director, producer and actor. Rita, whose real name was Margarita Carmen Cansino, was born in New York City.

(1946) CONSTANCE MOORE (*left*) and CONSTANCE BENNETT might have sold more toothpaste with their joint smiles than all other TV actors combined. Always among the nation's best-dressed women, these film beauties attracted the attention of every other female present at Hollywood parties. During her heyday in motion pictures, Miss Bennett was one of the screen's highest-paid leading ladies.

(1958)   PETER LAWFORD and his former wife, PAT KENNEDY, sister of the late President John F. Kennedy, were among the notables enjoying an evening's fun at the Moulin Rouge. The British-born actor and his wife became the parents of two children during their marriage. Pat's father, Joseph Kennedy, was United States Ambassador to Lawford's native England.

(1946) AVA GARDNER and former husband ARTIE SHAW were a happy twosome at this Hollywood nightclub. Following her brief marriage to the popular bandleader, Ava went on to become one of the screen's most sought-after leading ladies. Now living overseas, she is seldom seen in Hollywood these days. Shaw was also wed to another film beauty, Lana Turner.

(1956) ANNE BANCROFT was unable to control her laughter—listening to a jokester during a rest period on the set of *Apache Agent*, in which she played an Indian maiden. Anne, whose real name is Anna Maria Italiana, was born in the Bronx of Italian parentage. Hollywood tendered her an Oscar for her performance in *The Miracle Worker* in 1962. She enacted the same role on Broadway.

(1952) ZSA ZSA GABOR and her late husband, GEORGE SANDERS, were being interviewed by a radio reporter in this photo at a special showing of a new motion picture in Hollywood. Leading man of numerous motion pictures, the Russian-born actor received an Oscar in 1950 for his role in *All About Eve*. Before becoming an actor, he was in the tobacco business in South America.

(1954)   KIRK DOUGLAS and his wife, ANNE, were having a ball in this shot taken at the Cocoanut Grove. One of the screen's foremost dramatic stars and father of actor Michael Douglas, Kirk sold newspapers, waited on tables and did exhibition wrestling. He served with the United States Navy during World War II. Kirk now heads up his own production company.

(1957) CESAR ROMERO (*left*) and RONALD REAGAN were having a hilarious time during a dinner party at Romanoff's. The attractive back at the right belongs to former actress Nancy Davis, Reagan's charming wife. Nancy forsook her own acting career when she became Mrs. Reagan.

Familiar Faces

(1957) ANN MILLER and MAURICE CHEVALIER were among many first-nighters at a performance of the *Ice Follies* in Hollywood. Often referred to as "Mr. Paris" during his lengthy career as an entertainer, Chevalier was nearing his seventh decade in show business at the time of his death in 1972 in his native Paris. Ann, one of the screen's top dance stars, also gained worldwide fame as Hollywood's leading "goodwill ambassador," visiting the four corners of the globe.

(1958) CHARLES BOYER and his wife, PAT PATTERSON, a former
actress, drew an ovation from throngs of movie fans when they
appeared at the Hollywood premiere of *Gigi*, a musical film starring
three of the French-born actor's countrymen—Maurice Chevalier,
Louis Jourdan and Leslie Caron.

(1958)   ANGIE DICKINSON and BUDDY EBSEN blended their voices in
song during a production lull on the set of *Northwest Passage,* an
action-filled television series in which they starred, Ebsen as a
Colonial ranger and Angie as a pioneer woman. Daughter of a
newspaper publisher, Angie was born in Kulm, North Dakota.
Buddy was an internationally famous dancing star before extending
his career to include acting.

(1949)   VAN HEFLIN and KATHARINE HEPBURN were table companions at an industry social function. Hepburn's initial screen performance in *A Bill of Divorcement* in 1933 left no doubt as to her acting ability. Born in Hartford, Connecticut, and educated at Bryn Mawr College in Pennsylvania, Kate has a Yankee accent that has become as familiar to moviegoers as the chiming of Big Ben is to Londoners. Heflin, too, was much admired for his film and stage performances—with an Oscar (for *Johnny Eager*) to bear out his acting excellence.

(1956) DALE EVANS watches as husband ROY ROGERS shapes a new
Western chapeau for her. Between them, they use dozens of the
colorful hats each year. In addition to making movies, the popular
pair kept busy with television and personal appearances. *The Roy
Rogers Show* was a TV success for many seasons. Roy was born in
Cincinnati, and his real name is Leonard Slye.

(1952) EZIO PINZA and OLIVIA DE HAVILLAND were on hand to honor Judy Garland at an industry testimonial dinner in Hollywood, hosted by the Friars Club. Pinza's brilliant singing and acting in *South Pacific,* one of Broadway's most successful musicals, will live forever in the memories of those theatergoers fortunate enough to have seen him.

(1953)   STEWART GRANGER and actress wife JEAN SIMMONS joined RICHARD BURTON and his wife, SYBIL, to witness the Academy Award presentations. Nominated for Oscars on numerous occasions during his lengthy starring career, and justly so, Burton has yet to win one. Born in Pontrhydfen, Wales, educated at Oxford, Burton started life as Richard Jenkins. Incidentally, Granger's real name is James Stewart. It's understandable why he changed it.

(1956) ELIZABETH TAYLOR is shown with MICHAEL TODD, attending a film premiere in Beverly Hills shortly before they were wed. Her brief marriage to Todd was the third for the beautiful actress. Head over heels in love with Elizabeth, Todd met a tragic death in an airplane accident in 1958, a short time after marrying her. He produced one of Hollywood's all-time great films, *Around the World in 80 Days*.

(1950) SIR LAURENCE OLIVIER and his late wife, VIVIEN LEIGH, seen attending a gala party honoring them in Beverly Hills. England's gifts to Hollywood, both were awarded Oscars for their acting excellence. Her performances in *Gone With the Wind* and *A Streetcar Named Desire* accounted for two golden statuettes. His superb acting in *Hamlet* in 1948 won Olivier an Oscar as well. The titled, multi-talented actor is also a stage and film director and producer.

(1964) SIDNEY POITIER, ANNE BANCROFT and GREGORY PECK (*from left to right*) hurried backstage to be photographed at the Thirty-sixth Annual Awards Presentation of the American Academy of Motion Picture Arts and Sciences, in Santa Monica. Themselves Oscar winners, Anne and Greg presented Poitier with his own for his performance in *Lilies of the Field*. The Miami-born Poitier's screen performances have all been of award-winning quality.

(1953)   GLORIA SWANSON sat beside the late EARL WARREN during a supper party at Romanoff's. Once the Governor of California, Warren also served as Chief Justice of the Supreme Court of the United States. One of the all-time greats, Gloria began her lengthy popularity as a screen star in 1913, bridging the gap between silent films and the early talkies. She also attracted attention year after year as one of the world's best-dressed women, which she continues to be.

(1952) GREER GARSON (*left*) and GAIL PATRICK had things to discuss at a Damon Runyon Benefit Dinner in Hollywood. Gail, aside from her reputation as the movies' most attractive "other woman" in a number of films, also gained fame and fortune as the producer of top-rated television shows, particularly *Perry Mason*. A true Southern belle, Gail was born in Birmingham, Alabama. Her real name is Margaret Fitzpatrick.

(1961) SAMMY DAVIS, JR., and former wife MAY BRITT attend an opening-night performance at the Cocoanut Grove. Sammy, born in Harlem, New York, has endless talent. A dancer from earliest childhood, a member of an act that included his dad and uncle, he is also a great vocalist, musician and actor. Without question, he's a "one-man-show." May is the mother of his two children.

(1944)   HATTIE MCDANIEL, BRIGADIER GENERAL BENJAMIN O. DAVIS
and LENA HORNE (*from left to right*) found things to discuss during a
garden party honoring General Davis at the home of Ira Gershwin,
famed lyricist. Three hundred stars, producers and executives honored the army general—in Southern California for a tour of
inspection. An excellent actress, Hattie was awarded an Oscar for
her magnificent performance in *Gone With the Wind* in 1939.

(1953)   AUDREY HEPBURN and the late WILLIAM HOLDEN wait their turn to be introduced to some visiting royalty at a Hollywood reception. A very talented pair, Audrey and Bill won top acting honors in the same year—1953, she for *Roman Holiday,* he for *Stalag 17*. Born in Brussels, Audrey is one of the film industry's most popular stars. Holden was a native of O'Fallon, Illinois, his real name was William Franklin Beedle.

(1947) MYRNA LOY and her former husband, GENE MARKEY, a film producer, in their chauffeur-driven car as they departed from Restaurant LaRue. Their wraps and gloves bear out the fact that nights do get chilly in sunny California. The actress has always spent long hours in makeup, covering the freckles that have adorned her famous face since her earliest childhood in Helena, Montana, her birthplace.

(1955)   MARLENE DIETRICH and British actor MICHAEL RENNIE were
a surprise twosome at Ciro's. The always beautiful Marlene dated
many of the screen's handsomest leading men during her lengthy
career in Hollywood. None of her romances were ever taken
seriously—because she was the wife of Rudolph Sieber since her
debut as an actress in her native Berlin, Germany.

(1958) GARY COOPER's wife, ROCKY, points out a possible picture to the late screen star during a colorful dinner party. Coop was an excellent amateur photographer—fond of snapping candid pictures of his friends. Rocky was an actress at the time of her marriage to Cooper in 1933, and changed her name to Sandra Shaw for the movies. Samuel Goldwyn recognized Coop's acting ability very early.

(1951) BETTE DAVIS and her former husband, GARY MERRILL, attend an awards banquet in the Crystal Room of the Beverly Hills Hotel. Bette knows all about awards—Hollywood presented her with two Oscars for her acting excellence, in 1935 for *Dangerous* and in 1938 for *Jezebel*.

(1953)   HENRY FONDA chatted with tennis ace MAUREEN CONNOLLY during a party in Beverly Hills. One of the greatest players ever to wield a tennis racket, San Diego-born Maureen began winning honors from the time she was a youngster. Fonda, too, is an ace in his chosen profession, the star of countless stage and screen productions and winner of the 1982 Oscar for Best Actor. His offspring, Jane and Peter, have followed in his footsteps.

(1950)   RICHARD WIDMARK, shown with his wife, JEAN, a prominent screenwriter whom he wed in 1942, used a muffled whistle to attract the attention of a friend while waiting for the curtain to rise on a new Hollywood offering. An immediate success in his initial screen role, Widmark, a native of Sunrise, Minnesota, was an instructor of speech and dramatics at Lake Forest University, his alma mater, before seeking an acting career.

(1955) GRACE KELLY topped off her screen acting career by winning an Oscar for her 1954 performance in *The Country Girl*. Soon after, the Philadelphia-born actress became the bride of Prince Rainier of Monaco, with every producer in Hollywood wishing she would continue in films. The blue-eyed, blond princess also left a number of broken hearts behind.